GROWING CANNABIS

A comprehensive manual on cultivating marijuana for both recreational and therapeutic purposes

Oliver Wrench

Table of Contents

GROWING CANNABIS 1

Introduction 7

Chapter One 10

    Introduction: Basic Cannabis Botany and Overview of Cannabis Cultivation 10

Chapter Two 19

    Growing Cannabis 19

        Growing cannabis indoors: Advantages and Disadvantages 19

        Growing cannabis outdoors: Advantages and Disadvantages 25

Chapter Three 31

   How to setup a grow area to cultivate cannabis 31

   Germination and Seedling Stage 37

Chapter Four 44

   Vegetative stage for cannabis 44

   Flowering stage for cannabis 49

Chapter Five 55

   Cannabis harvesting 55

   Cannabis drying and curing 60

Chapter Six 65

Troubleshooting 10 common problems associated with growing cannabis 65

Chapter Seven 75

Medical and Recreational Use of Cannabis 75

Medical Usage of Cannabis 75

Cannabis Usage for Recreation 77

Health Effects of cannabis: Short-term, long-term, psychological impact and physical health concerns .. 80

ACKNOWLEDGEMENTS 84

Copyright © 2024 by Oliver Wrench

All rights reserved. No part of this publication may be reproduced, distributed, or transmitted in any form or by any means, including photocopying, recording, or other electronic or mechanical methods, without the prior written permission of the publisher, except in the case of brief quotations embodied in critical reviews and certain other non-commercial uses permitted by copyright law.

DISCLAIMER

This information is not intended to provide medical advice or substitute for the advice or treatment of a personal physician. It is suggested that you get counsel from your doctors or skilled health professionals regarding any particular health concerns you may have. Readers and followers of this educational resource are responsible for any potential health consequences.

Introduction

Discover the techniques for successfully developing your personal cannabis garden with Oliver Wrench's innovative guide, "Growing Cannabis." Whether you possess extensive experience in cultivating cannabis or are a beginner seeking knowledge, this book serves as your ultimate guide to achieving mastery in the intricate and scientific process of cannabis production.

Imagine the process of converting a basic seed into a flourishing plant, abundant with aromatic buds and potent compounds.

"Growing Cannabis" provides comprehensive knowledge on the technical aspects of planting, caring for, and harvesting, as well as valuable insights derived from extensive hands-on experience and focused research.

Oliver Wrench, a highly esteemed authority in the field of cannabis production, elucidates the process by providing explicit and step-by-step guidance that vividly depicts every stage of growth.

However, "Growing Cannabis" transcends being merely an instructional guide. It is a celebration of the plant itself, encompassing its diverse applications and significant influence on the field of medicine. The author's passion for cannabis is apparent throughout the entire book, motivating readers not just to cultivate it but also to recognize the profound qualities and possibilities of this extraordinary plant.

Join the multitude of readers who have transformed their gardens into flourishing, verdant sanctuaries. If you have an interest in cultivating cannabis for personal use, medical purposes, or as part of a business venture,

"Growing Cannabis" is the indispensable manual that will boost your growing abilities and deepen your understanding of this wonderful plant.

Explore the book "Growing Cannabis" by Oliver Wrench now and begin a voyage of cultivation, exploration, and boundless opportunities in the world of cannabis.

Chapter One

Introduction: Basic Cannabis Botany and Overview of Cannabis Cultivation

For thousands of years, people have grown the flowering plant genus Cannabis for a variety of functions, including industrial, recreational, and medical applications. Within this genus, *Cannabis sativa*, *Cannabis indica*, and *Cannabis ruderalis* are the most well-known species.

TAXONOMY AND CLASSIFICATION

Kingdom: Plantae

Clade: Angiosperms

Clade: Eudicots

Order: Rosales

Family: Cannabaceae

Genus: Cannabis

MORPHOLOGY

Roots:

- Just like a keen observer of nature, it's fascinating to note that cannabis plants possess a taproot system accompanied by lateral roots. Just as a plant relies on its roots to secure its position and extract essential resources from the soil, it is crucial for the roots to fulfill these vital functions.

Stem:

- The stem is strong and may contain either hollow space or pith. It plays a crucial role in supporting the plant and facilitating the transportation of nutrients and water from the roots to the leaves.

Leaves:

- The leaves of cannabis plants usually have a palmate shape and serrated edges. They consist of multiple leaflets, typically ranging from 5 to 9 leaflets per leaf. The leaves grow directly across from one another on the stem, arranged in an opposite phyllotaxy.

Flowers:

- Due to its dioecious nature, cannabis has separate male and female plants.
- *Male Flowers:* They are smaller in size and consist of clusters of pollen sacs. They generate pollen that fertilizes female flowers.
- *Female Flowers:* These are responsible for producing the resinous buds that contain cannabinoids like THC and CBD. Female flowers possess pistils that efficiently collect pollen from male plants.

Trichomes:

- These small structures are commonly located on the flowers and can also be found on the leaves and stems to a lesser degree. Trichomes play a crucial role in the production and storage of cannabinoids and terpenes, which are responsible for the plant's psychoactive and aromatic properties.

CANNABINOIDS AND TERPENES

Cannabinoids:

- Tetrahydrocannabinol (THC) and cannabidiol (CBD) are two of the main types of cannabinoids. THC is responsible for the psychoactive effects, whereas CBD is renowned for its medicinal properties without inducing a euphoric state.

Terpenes:

- These are aromatic chemicals that give plants their flavor and smell. Furthermore, terpenes can interact with cannabinoids, thereby amplifying their effects through a phenomenon known as the "entourage effect."

LIFE CYCLE

Germination:

- Seed germination is the first stage of the process, during which the seed takes in water, expands, and sprouts a taproot. Seedling: Once the seed has sprouted, the plant moves into the seedling phase, where it starts to grow its initial set of true leaves.

Vegetative Stage:

- During this stage, the plant prioritizes the growth of its leaves, stems, and roots. This stage thrives on abundant light and nutrients, which are essential for developing a robust structure to support the flowering process.

Flowering Stage:

- When the plant experiences a shift in light exposure, typically a decrease to 12 hours of light per day, it undergoes a transition to the flowering stage, resulting in the production of beautiful flowers. During the flowering stage, which spans several weeks, female plants undergo bud development, resulting in the accumulation of cannabinoids.

Harvest:

- After the flowers reach maturity, they undergo the necessary steps of harvesting, drying, and curing in order to be ready for consumption or further processing.

CULTIVATION AND CARE

Light:

- For optimal growth, cannabis plants need ample amounts of light, especially during the vegetative stage, where they thrive with 16–24 hours of light per day. During the flowering stage, they can do well with slightly less light, around 12 hours per day.

Water:

- Proper watering is essential, ensuring that the soil remains well-drained. Ensuring proper drainage is crucial in order to avoid the occurrence of root rot.

Nutrients:

- For cannabis to thrive, it requires a well-rounded combination of essential nutrients such as nitrogen, phosphorus, potassium, and trace elements.

Temperature and humidity:

- The ideal temperature range is between 20 and 30 °C (68 and 86 °F) during the day, with slightly cooler temperatures at night. It is important to maintain moderate humidity levels during vegetative growth and lower levels during flowering in order to avoid the development of mold and mildew.

Having a solid understanding of cannabis botany is crucial for successful cultivation and optimizing the plant's yield and quality.

COMPARING SOIL AND HYDROPONICS

- **Soil:** richer in organic content, more forgiving, and easier for novices to work with.

- **Hydroponics:** more yields and faster growth, but it's more complicated and needs precise fertilizer control.

MANAGEMENT OF INSECTS AND DISEASES

- **Prevention:** Use good soil, maintain a clean growing environment, and frequently check on your plants.
- **Most Common Problems:** Powdery mildew, aphids, spider mites, and root rot.
- **Solutions:** proper airflow, natural predators, and organic pesticides.

LEGAL CONSIDERATIONS

- **Regulations:** vary greatly depending on the area. Comprehending and adhering to regional regulations pertaining to cannabis growing is vital.

Chapter Two

Growing Cannabis

Cannabis cultivation indoors is becoming increasingly popular due to its ability to regulate the climate and improve growing conditions. This is a thorough instruction on growing cannabis indoors, including the advantages and disadvantages of the technique.

Growing cannabis indoors: Advantages and Disadvantages

1. PREPARE THE GROWING SPACE.

- **Select an Appropriate Location:** Pick a location that is both covert and convenient, like a grow tent, closet, or extra room.

- **Lightproof the Space:** Make sure that during the dark periods of the plant's light cycle, no light is leaking in or out.

2. PICK THE APPROPRIATE TOOLS.

- **Grow lights:** Common options are LED, HPS (High-Pressure Sodium), and CFL (Compact Fluorescent Lights). LED lighting uses less energy and generates less heat.

- **Ventilation System:** To control humidity and temperature, install oscillating fans, intake fans, and exhaust fans.

- **Grow Medium:** Soil, hydroponic systems, or coco coir can be used. While growing on soil is easier for beginners, hydroponics can produce faster results.

- **Containers:** Make use of well-drained pots. For root aeration, fabric pots, also known as smart pots, are helpful.

- **Nutrients:** Get nutrients that are designed especially for cannabis and adhere to feeding plans for the various growth stages (vegetative, flowering, and seedling).

3. GERMINATE SEEDS AND PLANT SEEDLINGS.

- **Germination:** Use a paper towel or place seeds directly in a growing medium.

- **Planting:** Place seeds or seedlings in the grow medium of your choice after they have germinated.

4. CONTROL THE LIGHT CYCLES.

- **Vegetative Stage:** 18 to 24 hours of light each day.

- **Flowering Stage:** To encourage flowering, switch to 12 hours of light and 12 hours of darkness.

5. MAINTAIN IDEAL CONDITIONS.

- **Temperature:** Keep daytime temperatures between 70 and 85°F (20 and 30°C) and nighttime temperatures slightly cooler.

- **Humidity:** Maintain a humidity level of 40–70%, greater when in the vegetative stage and less when in flower.

- **Watering:** Give plants water when the soil feels dry in the top inch. Make sure there is enough drainage to avoid root rot.

6. MONITOR THE HEALTH OF THE PLANT.

- **Pests and diseases:** Observe plants frequently for indications of pests and illnesses. Utilize natural or chemical treatments as needed.

- **Pruning and Training:** To maximize light exposure and productivity, trim extra foliage and apply methods like topping, LST (Low-Stress Training), and SCROG (Screen of Green).

7. HARVESTING.

- **Timing:** Harvest when the trichomes (resin glands) are milky white or amber.

- **Curing and drying:** To dry, hang the collected buds in a place that is cool, dark, and well-ventilated. Cure for several weeks in sealed jars to enhance flavor and potency.

Advantages of Growing Cannabis Indoors

- **Environmental Control:** The capacity to regulate CO_2 levels, temperature, light, and humidity to provide ideal growing conditions.

- **Year-Round Cultivation:** Seasonal variations have no effect on indoor cultivation, unlike outdoor cultivation.

- **Privacy and Security:** Growing indoors provides greater seclusion and safety, which lowers the possibility of theft or unwelcome attention.

- **Management of Pests and Diseases:** It is simpler to maintain indoor surroundings clean and to control diseases and pests more successfully.

- **Improved Quality Control:** A greater ability to monitor and regulate the strength and quality of the cannabis produced.

Disadvantages of Growing Cannabis Indoors

- **High Initial Costs:** When cultivating indoors, setups for lighting, ventilation, and other equipment can be costly.

- **Energy Consumption:** Growing inside uses a lot of electricity, especially for climate management and lights.

- **Limited Space:** The quantity and size of plants that can be grown indoors may be limited.

- **Technical expertise:** Proper management of indoor growth environments and plant care necessitates knowledge and experience.

- **Maintenance:** To guarantee ideal circumstances and plant health, indoor setups need to be regularly maintained and observed.

Indoor cannabis cultivation has some benefits in terms of quality and control, but it also requires higher costs and more care. Indoor growth can be a very productive method of cultivating cannabis for people who are prepared to put in the effort and the financial resources.

Growing cannabis outdoors: Advantages and Disadvantages

Cultivating cannabis outdoors may be a profitable and rewarding venture. Here's a guide on growing cannabis outside, including the advantages and disadvantages of the approach.

1. SELECT THE APPROPRIATE SITE.

- **Sunlight:** Choose an area that gets at least 6 to 8 hours of direct sunlight per day.

- **Security:** To avoid theft and unwanted attention, make sure the space is secure and not readily accessible to the public.

- **Accessibility:** Pick a location that will be easy to water and care for.

2. PICK THE APPROPRIATE STRAINS.

- **Climate Suitability:** Select strains that are appropriate for the weather in your area. While Sativa strains do better in warmer settings, Indica strains tend to be more resilient and able to survive in colder climates.

- **Autoflowering strains:** They can be simpler for novices and are less reliant on light cycles.

3. GET THE SOIL READY.

- **Soil Quality:** Choose high-quality, organic-rich soil. To increase the amount of nutrients in the soil, amend it using compost, manure, or commercial fertilizers.

- **pH Level:** Keep the soil pH between 6.0 and 7.0. Check the soil and add lime or sulfur if needed.

4. PLANTING

- **Germination:** Seeds should be sown indoors or in a greenhouse, and they should be transplanted outdoors once they have been sufficiently developed.

- **Spacing:** Give seeds or seedlings enough room to grow.

It is generally advised to space them 3–6 feet apart.

5. NUTRIENTS AND WATERING

- **Watering:** Give plants regular watering, especially in arid weather. Make sure the soil is still damp but not soggy.

- **Nutrients:** Provide plants with the right nutrients at the right times of growth. During the vegetative stage, use fertilizers high in nitrogen; during the flowering stage, use nutrients high in phosphorus.

6. PEST AND DISEASE MANAGEMENT

- **Inspection:** Frequently check plants for indications of illness or pests.

- **Natural Predators:** To keep pests under control, promote beneficial insects like ladybugs and predatory mites.

- **Organic Solutions:** Use neem oil, insecticidal soaps, or other organic treatments if necessary.

7. TRAINING AND PRUNING

- **FIMing and topping:** FIMing, or chopping off the main stem, is one technique that can encourage bushier growth.

- **Pruning:** To increase air circulation and light penetration, remove dead or yellowing leaves and lower branches.

8. HARVESTING

- **Timing:** For maximum potency, harvest when the trichomes are amber or milky white.

- **Drying and Curing:** Place buds in a cool, dark place with good ventilation. Cure for a few weeks in sealed jars to improve taste and potency.

Advantages of Growing Cannabis Outdoors

- **Reduced Costs:** Growing outdoors does not require costly lighting or ventilation systems.

- **Natural sunlight:** The complete spectrum of sunlight is beneficial to plants and can result in strong development and increased yields.

- **Eco-Friendly:** Because outdoor growing uses less energy, it has a smaller negative influence on the environment.

- **Greater Plant Sizes and Yields:** Plants can grow larger and yield more when given enough room and favorable environmental circumstances.

- **Simplicity:** Compared to indoor growth, outdoor gardening requires less setup and upkeep.

Disadvantages of Growing Cannabis Outdoors

- **Environmental Factors:** Weather-related events like wind, rain, and temperature swings can have an impact on a plant's ability to grow and produce.

- **Diseases and Pests:** Managing increased exposure to diseases, animals, and pests can be difficult.

- **Security and privacy:** Since outdoor plants are more noticeable, they may be stolen or vandalized.

- **Limited Growing Season:** The number of harvests per year may be restricted due to a limited growing season, which is dependent on the climate.

- **Less Control:** Compared to indoor growth, outside gardening provides less control over environmental elements that can impact the crop's consistency and quality.

Growing cannabis outdoors has the potential to be a high-yielding, economical, and environmentally beneficial alternative. But there are drawbacks as well, such as weather exposure, pests, and security concerns. For both new and seasoned growers, outdoor cultivation may be a fulfilling experience if the proper strains are selected and the growing environment is properly managed.

Chapter Three

How to setup a grow area to cultivate cannabis

To guarantee that the plants have the best growing circumstances possible, cannabis cultivation requires meticulous preparation and attention to detail while setting up a growing environment. To get you started, consider the following thorough guide:

SELECT THE SITE

Space: Choose an area that may be devoted to growing, such as a closet, tent, or room. Ensure that you can seal it to control the atmosphere and that it is easily accessible.

Size: Choose the appropriate size based on how many plants you intend to cultivate. A 4 × 4 foot area is usually good for 4-6 plants.

Ventilation: In this location, there should be enough ventilation and exhaust.

PREPARE THE GROWING AREA.

Cleanliness: To avoid mold and vermin, make sure the area is tidy.

Reflective Material: To optimize light efficiency, line the walls with Mylar or other reflective materials.

Sealing: To regulate the light cycle, make the place light-proof.

LIGHTING

Types of lighting:

LEDs: low heat output and energy efficiency.

HID (High-Intensity Discharge): The vegetative stage uses MH (Metal Halide), while the flowering stage uses HPS (High-Pressure Sodium). Compact fluorescent lights, or CFLs, work well in small, growing areas.

Light Cycle: The flowering stage needs 12 hours of light and 12 hours of darkness, whereas the vegetative stage needs 18 to 24 hours of light.

Distance: To avoid scorching or stretching, adjust the light's height based on the plant's growth stage.

AIRFLOW AND VENTILATION

Inline Fan and Ducting: To exhaust hot air and introduce fresh air, use an inline fan and ducting.

Carbon Filter: To reduce odor, fit a carbon filter to the exhaust.

Oscillating Fans: To promote airflow and strengthen the plants, install fans in the grow area.

CONTROL OF HUMIDITY AND TEMPERATURE

Thermometer and hygrometer: Ensure you keep an eye on the relative humidity and temperature.

Heater/AC: To maintain ideal temperatures (70–85°F

during the day and 58–70°F at night), use a heater or air conditioner.

Humidifier/Dehumidifier: To maintain ideal humidity levels (40–60% for the majority of the development cycle), use a humidifier or dehumidifier

GROWING MEDIUM

Soil: For improved drainage, use premium organic soil that has preferably been combined with perlite.

Soilless Mix: Options such as peat moss or coco coir.

Hydroponics: increasing yields and speeding up growth by cultivating plants in a nutrient-rich water solution.

WATERING AND NUTRIENTS

Nutrients: Use cannabis-specific nutrients. Larger quantities of phosphorus and potassium are typically required during blooming, while larger levels of nitrogen are typically required during the vegetative stage.

pH Level: For soil, maintain the pH of the water and fertilizer solution between 6.0 and 7.0; for hydroponics, keep it between 5.5 and 6.5.

Watering: Avoid excessive watering. Give the plants frequent, thorough waterings, letting the top inch of soil dry out in between.

TRAINING FOR PLANTS

Topping and FIMing: cutting the plant's top to encourage bushier growth.

Low-Stress Training (LST): To build an even canopy, bend and tie branches down.

Scrogging (Screen of Green): training plants horizontally with a screen.

CONTROL OF PESTS AND DISEASES

Preventive Measures: Conduct routine plant inspections, maintain cleanliness in the vicinity, and employ natural repellents.

Treatment: If pests are found, apply insecticidal soaps or organic pesticides.

HARVESTING AND CURING

Harvest Time: Harvest when there is some amber and the trichomes are milky white.

Drying: Hang the plants upside down in a dark, well-ventilated room with temperatures ranging from 65 to 75°F and 50% humidity.

Curing: After the buds have dried, put them in airtight jars and, for the first few weeks, open them every day to let the moisture out to promote curing.

You can be assured of healthy growth and optimize the yield of your cannabis plants by correctly setting up and maintaining your grow area.

Germination and Seedling Stage

In cannabis growing, the germination and seedling stages are crucial. Using the right methods at these phases guarantees robust, healthy plants. Here's a comprehensive guide to help you through these early stages:

GERMINATION STAGE

Materials Needed:

- Cannabis seeds

- Tap or distilled water (dechlorinated by leaving it out for 24 hours)

- Either a germination kit or paper towels are required.

- You will need two plastic containers with lids or two plates.

- pH meter or pH strips (optional)

Techniques:

Paper Towel Technique:

- **Soak the seeds:** To hydrate the seeds, soak them in a glass of water for 12 to 24 hours. They should sink to the bottom, suggesting that they are prepared for the next phase.
- **Get the paper towels ready:** Use distilled water to wet two paper towels. They should be somewhat damp, but not drenched.
- **Arrange the Seeds:** Disperse the seeds onto a damp paper towel. Put the second paper towel over them.
- **Create a dark environment:** To create a dark, humid environment, place the paper towels with seeds between two plates or in a lidded plastic container.
- **Check Frequently:** Check the seeds every day and keep the paper towels moist. The seeds should produce taproots in 1–7 days.

Direct Soil Technique:

- **Prepare the soil:** Use a light potting mix or seed starter soil. Make sure it is damp but not waterlogged.
- **Plant the seeds:** Dig a small hole in the soil, about 0.25–0.5 inches deep. After planting the seed in the hole, gently cover it with soil.
- **Watering:** To keep the soil moist, water it gently. Take caution not to overwater.
- **Temperature and Light:** Until the seedlings sprout, keep the soil warm (between 70 and 85°F) and provide indirect light.

SEEDLING STAGE

Materials Needed:

- Small pots or seedling trays

- Growing media, such as coco coir or seed starter soil, is essential.

- Humidity Dome (optional) Grow lamps (LEDs or CFLs)

- Thermometer and hygrometer

STEPS:

1. Transplanting Sprouted Seeds:

- **Prepare the Pots:** Use a light, well-draining growth material to fill small pots or seedling trays.
- **Plant the Seeds:** After the seeds have sprouted taproots, carefully transfer them to the pots that have been prepared. With the taproot facing downward, place a thin layer of soil over it.
- **Watering:** Don't overwater the soil; just keep it damp. To keep the fragile roots from being disturbed, use a spray bottle.

2. Environment:

- **Temperature:** Keep the temperature between 70 and 85 degrees Fahrenheit (21 and 29 degrees Celsius).

- **Humidity:** During the seedling stage, maintain humidity levels between 65 and 70 percent. Maintaining these levels can be aided by a humidity dome.

- **Lighting:** Make sure there is light available 18–24 hours a day. The grow lamps should be positioned 2-4 inches above the seedlings. As the seedlings get bigger, adjust the height to avoid burning or straining them.

GROWTH AND CARE:

- **Air circulation:** Ensure sufficient air movement to fortify the stems and prevent mold growth. A tiny oscillating fan may be useful.

- **Monitoring:** Keep an eye out for any indications of mold, pests, or nutritional shortages. Seedlings should grow steadily and have a bright green color.

- **Watering and Nutrients:** When the top inch of soil appears dry, water the seedlings. Don't overwater. The seedlings don't need a lot of extra nutrients at this point. To prevent nutrient burn, use a nutrient solution at 1/4 strength if you are using one.

Transplanting to bigger pots:

- **Timing:** Transplant the seedlings when they have 3–4 true leaves and their roots begin to outgrow the seedling tray or small pots.
- **Process for Transplanting:** Carefully remove the seedlings from their pots so as not to damage the roots. Put them in bigger pots that have been completely filled with the selected growing material and watered.

You may provide your cannabis plants with a solid foundation for healthy growth throughout their lifecycle by following these instructions throughout the germination and seedling stages.

Chapter Four

Vegetative stage for cannabis

Cannabis plants concentrate on developing a robust root system and producing beautiful foliage while in the vegetative stage. Here is a comprehensive guide to successfully managing the vegetative stage:

ENVIRONMENTAL CONDITIONS:

Lighting:

- Provide 18 to 24 hours of light daily. Fluorescent, HID (metal halide), or LED lighting are frequently utilized in this phase.

- For best growth, keep the light intensity between 400 and 600 µmol/m2/s.

Temperature:

- Throughout the day, keep the temperature between 70

and 85°F (21 and 29°C).

- At night, the temperature may drop to between 60 and 70 °F (15 and 21 °C).

- Avoid excessive temperature changes.

Humidity:

- Maintain a humidity range of 40–70%.

- Higher humidity (60–70%) encourages faster growth, whereas lower humidity (40–60%) helps avoid mildew and mold.

Air Circulation:

- To avoid stagnant air and reduce the risk of pests and diseases, make sure there is adequate air movement throughout the grow area.

- To gently move air around the plants, use oscillating fans.

NUTRIENTS AND WATERING:

Nutrients:

- During this stage, use a balanced fertilizer that has a higher nitrogen (N) content to encourage the growth of foliage.

- Adhere to the dilution and application directions provided by the manufacturer.

- For a more natural method, think about utilizing organic nutrients.

Watering:

- When the top inch of soil seems dry, water the plants.

- Prevent overwatering, as this might cause other issues such as root rot.

- Proper drainage is essential to preventing waterlogging.

pH Level:

- For soil systems, keep the pH of the water and fertilizer solution between 6.0 and 7.0; for hydroponic systems, keep it between 5.5 and 6.5.

- pH changes can impact the absorption of nutrients, so monitor and adjust as necessary on a regular basis.

TRAINING AND PRUNING:

Topping:

- In order to promote lateral growth and produce a bushier plant, topping entails cutting off the top growth tip of the main stem.

- This process is usually carried out once the plant has produced 4 to 6 pairs of true leaves.

FIMing:

- FIMing provides a less forceful alternative to topping. Instead of eliminating the entire new growth tip, only a piece of it is removed.

- This process promotes the development of several new branches.

Low-Stress Training (LST):

- LST entails gently bending and tying down branches to provide a more equal canopy.

- This method encourages more consistent growth and helps maximize light exposure to lower branches.

MONITORING AND CARE:

Management of Pests and Diseases:

- Check plants frequently for symptoms of diseases (like powdery mildew and bud rot) and pests (like spider mites and aphids).

- Use organic pest management measures whenever possible to reduce chemical exposure.

Support:

- To keep larger plants or those with heavy buds from bending or breaking under their own weight, provide support in the form of trellises or stakes.

Monitoring Growth:

- Monitor the growth of the plants and adjust the environment and nutrition levels as necessary.

- Monitor the total number of nodes and the general health of the plant.

By following these guidelines, you can help your cannabis plants thrive during the vegetative stage, paving the way for a healthy and productive flowering phase.

Flowering stage for cannabis

Cannabis plants go from concentrating on vegetative growth to generating flowers (buds) that are high in terpenes and cannabinoids during the flowering period. Here's a comprehensive guide to successfully handling the flowering stage:

LIGHT CYCLE:

Transitioning to Flowering:

- Change the light cycle to 12 hours of continuous light followed by 12 hours of darkness to start flowering.

- To prevent light interruptions during the dark period, which can interfere with the flowering process, make sure the area is completely dark.

Consider Lighting:

- Make use of premium grow lights designed for flowering, such as HPS (High-Pressure Sodium) or LED lights whose spectrum is tailored for flowering.

- Keep the light intensity between 600 and 1000 μmol/m2/s for the best bud development.

ENVIRONMENTAL CONDITIONS:

Temperature:

- Throughout the day, keep the temperature between 65 and 80 °F (18 and 27 °C).

- Nighttime temperatures can decrease to roughly 55–75°F

(13–24°C).

- Avoid extreme temperature swings, as they might cause stress to plants and interfere with the growth of buds.

Humidity:

- Lower the humidity to between 40 and 50 percent throughout the flowering period to avoid mold and bud rot.

- In order to manage humidity levels and avoid moisture buildup, proper ventilation and air movement are important.

NUTRIENTS AND WATERING:

Nutrient Requirements:

- To stimulate flower development, switch to a bloom-specific nutrient mix with higher phosphorus (P) and potassium (K) content.

- For nutrient dosing, adhere to the manufacturer's instructions and modify in light of the plant's requirements and reaction.

Watering:

- Water the plants as needed, making sure the growing medium or soil is continuously moist but not waterlogged.

- Refrain from overwatering since it might cause nutritional imbalances and other root issues.

pH Level:

- Water and nutrient solutions should have pH values that are monitored and kept within the proper range (6.0–7.0 for soil, 5.5–6.5 for hydroponic systems).

- pH changes must be regularly monitored and adjusted because they can impact nutrient uptake and overall plant health.

TRAINING AND PRUNING:

Defoliation:

- Eliminate oversized fan leaves that obstruct light from

reaching lower bud sites.

- Defoliation should be done sparingly and carefully because the plant still needs some leaves for photosynthesis and nutrient uptake.

Support:

- To help sustain heavy buds and keep branches from bending or breaking under their weight, add extra support in the form of trellises or plant stakes.

MONITORING AND CARE:

Management of Pests and Diseases:

- Even during the flowering period, plants might still be threatened by pests and diseases, so keep an eye out for them.

- Reduce hazards by taking proactive steps and using organic pest control techniques, all without using dangerous chemicals on the flowers.

Flowering Progress:

- Keep track of bud growth and trichome production.

- The ideal cannabinoid and terpene profile will determine when to harvest, so pay close attention to the plants to ensure they are perfectly ripe.

Final Flush:

- When flowering is almost over, flush the plants with plain water to get rid of extra nutrients and enhance flavor and aroma.

- In order to give the plants enough time to use up any remaining nutrients before harvest, modify the watering and nutrient regimens accordingly.

You may encourage the growth of your cannabis plants throughout the flowering stage and produce high-quality buds with strong terpene and cannabinoid profiles by adhering to these rules.

Chapter Five

Cannabis harvesting

Timely harvesting of cannabis is essential to achieving optimal potency, flavor, and overall quality of the buds.

Here's a comprehensive guide to cannabis harvesting:

SIGNS OF READINESS:

Color of Trichome:

- Use a magnification tool such as a jeweler's loupe or a microscope to examine the trichomes, which are small resin glands, on the buds.

- Harvest your cannabis for a well-balanced THC and CBD high when the majority of trichomes have turned milky white or cloudy.

- Await the moment when certain trichomes turn amber for a more sedative effect.

Color of Pistil:

- Monitor the color of the pistils. As the plant ages, it will progressively turn from white to reddish-brown in color.

- When most pistils have darkened and begun to curl inward, harvest.

Density and size of buds:

- The buds of a mature plant will be dense, compact, and plump.

- Avoid picking buds too early while they are still tiny and airy.

HARVESTING PROCEDURE:

Preparation:

- Organize your workplace with hygienic supplies like gloves, pruning shears, sharp scissors, and containers to store the buds you've gathered.

- Clean your instruments and hands to avoid cross-contamination.

Selective Harvesting:

- Harvest the top buds (colas) first since they are the most mature.

- If the plant has many flowering sites, harvest the lower buds as they mature to allow for staggered harvesting.

Cutting:

- Carefully cut each branch just above the node where it joins the main stem using pruning shears or scissors.

- To reduce trichome damage, try not to handle the buds too much.

Trimming:

- Trim the buds of any extra leaves or stems.

- After cutting or after drying, this can be completed right away.

- For a well-groomed look, cut off the larger fan leaves but leave the tiny sugar leaves clinging to the buds for flavor and strength.

Drying:

- In a dark, well-ventilated space with a temperature range of 60–70°F (15–21°C) and a humidity level of 45–55 percent, hang the trimmed buds upside down.

- To ensure adequate airflow around each bud, hang the branches using drying racks or threads.

- The buds should be dried for 7–14 days, or until the stems snap rather than bend.

- Avoid over-drying since this might alter the flavor and potency.

Curing:

- Put the dried buds in glass jars or other airtight containers.

- Keep the jars somewhere dark and cool, with a

temperature range of 60–70°F (15–21°C) and a humidity range of 55–65%.

- For the first week, open the jars every day to let out excess moisture and encourage curing.

- For optimal curing, allow the buds to cure for a minimum of 2 to 4 weeks, occasionally opening the jars to avoid mold growth.

POST-HARVEST CARE:

Storage:

- After the buds are cured, keep them in airtight jars in a cool, dry place away from moisture, light, and heat.

- Buds that have been properly cured can keep their flavor and potency for several months or perhaps a year.

Quality control:

- Check for symptoms of pest infestation, mold, or mildew on stored buds on a regular basis.

- To avoid contaminating the remaining buds, remove any that are decaying or damaged.

By following these guidelines, you can harvest cannabis at the height of its flavor and potency, giving users a fulfilling and delightful experience.

Cannabis drying and curing

For cannabis to maintain its strength, flavor, and general quality, appropriate drying and curing are necessary. Here's a comprehensive guide to successfully drying and curing cannabis:

CANNABIS DRYING:

Harvest Timing:

- Harvest your cannabis for a balanced THC and CBD high when most of the trichomes have gone cloudy or milky white.

- Wait until some trichomes turn amber if you're looking for a more sedative effect.

Trimming:

- As soon as the buds are harvested, remove any extra leaves or stems.

- Keep the smaller sugar leaves clinging to the buds and remove the larger fan leaves to achieve a well-groomed look.

Hanging:

- In a dark, well-ventilated space with a temperature range of 60–70°F (15–21°C) and a humidity level of 45–55%, hang the trimmed buds upside down.

- To ensure adequate airflow around each bud, hang the branches using drying racks or threads.

- To prevent the growth of mold and mildew, it is important to ensure that the drying area is not overcrowded.

Monitoring:

- While the buds are drying, check them frequently. They need to feel somewhat damp inside but dry on the exterior.

- Drying may take 7 to 14 days, depending on the surroundings.

Testing:

- Bend the stems slightly to see if the buds are ready. The buds are dry enough when they snap rather than bend.

CANNABIS CURING:

Preparation:

- After the buds have dried, place them in airtight jars or other receptacles.

- If you want to cure in a controlled atmosphere, use firmly sealed containers.

First Stage of Curing:

- The jars should be kept in a cool, dark area with

temperatures between 60 and 70°F (15 and 21°C) and humidity levels between 55 and 65%.

- For the first week, open the jars every day to let out excess moisture and encourage curing.

- Using a hygrometer, check the humidity levels inside the jars and make any necessary adjustments by adding or removing humidity packs.

Burping:

- Every day, burp the jars by opening them for a few minutes to let new air in and let out any extra moisture.

- Over the next few weeks, as the buds continue to cure, gradually reduce the frequency of burping.

Curing Duration:

- Allow the flavors to develop and the cannabinoids to mature by curing the buds for a minimum of 2 to 4 weeks.
- Some growers choose to cure for extended lengths of time—up to several months—in order to attain the ideal

potency and taste.

Quality control:

- Check the cured buds frequently for indications of pest infestation, mold, or mildew.

- Eliminate any decaying or damaged buds to avoid contaminating the remaining ones.

Storage:

- After the buds are cured, keep them in airtight jars in a cool, dry place away from moisture, light, and heat.

- Buds that have been properly cured can keep their flavor and potency for several months or perhaps a year.

These instructions will help you make sure your cannabis is dried and cured correctly, producing buds that are strong, tasty, and delightful to consume.

Chapter Six

Troubleshooting 10 common problems associated with growing cannabis

Growing cannabis can come with a number of difficulties. Here are ten common issues and troubleshooting methods to resolve them:

1. NUTRIENT DEFICIENCIES

Symptoms:

- Leaf yellowing (nitrogen deficiency)

- Purple stems (Phosphorus deficiency)

- Leaf margins that are burnt or brown (potassium deficiency)

Leaf discoloration or spots (deficiency in calcium, magnesium, or other micronutrients).

Troubleshooting:

- **Soil testing:** Determine the pH of your soil or growing medium. Cannabis grows best at a pH of 6.0–7.0 in soil and 5.5–6.5 in hydroponics.
- **Balanced Fertilizers**: Use a balanced fertilizer made just for cannabis. Refer to the dosing guidelines provided by the manufacturer.
- **Supplementation:** Use nutrient supplements (e.g., Cal-Mag for calcium and magnesium) to correct specific deficiencies if deficiencies are proven.

2. LIGHT BURN OR LIGHT DEFICIENCY

Symptoms:

- **Light burn:** leaves with bleached, yellowed, or brown areas.

- **Light deficiency:** slow growth and stretching (plants becoming tall and lanky).

Troubleshooting:

- **Appropriate Distance:** Adjust the distance between the canopy and the lights. Make sure that high-intensity lights are not too close.
- **Light Schedule:** Set appropriate light schedules (18/6 light/dark for vegetative and 12/12 for flowering).
- **Reflective Surfaces:** To optimize light efficacy, incorporate reflective surfaces into the cultivation area.

3. OVERWATERING AND UNDERWATERING

Symptoms:

- Overwatering can result in withering, yellowing leaves, and root rot.

- Underwatering can result in wilting, dry, and brittle leaves.

Troubleshooting:

- **Watering routine:** Set up and adhere to a regular watering routine. Water well, but let the top inch of soil dry out in between applications.

- **Drainage:** To avoid waterlogging, make sure pots have enough drainage. Fabric pots are a viable option as they offer superior aeration.

- **Monitoring:** To determine when your plants want watering, use a soil moisture meter.

4. MILDEW AND MOLD

Symptoms:

- White powdery substance on the leaves (powdery mildew).

- Grayish mold on buds (Bud rot)

Troubleshooting:

- **Controlling humidity:** Keep the right amount of humidity at 40–50% during the vegetative stage and 30–40% during the flowering stage.

- **Air Circulation:** Use fans and adequate ventilation to ensure adequate air circulation.
- **Pruning:** To increase airflow around plants, trim lower branches and leaves.
- **Fungicides:** If mold or mildew develops, apply organic fungicides.

5. SLOW OR INHIBITED GROWTH

Symptoms:

- Plants appear small and do not grow as anticipated.

Troubleshooting:

- **Environment:** Make sure that the temperature, humidity, light, and ventilation are ideal for growing.
- **Nutrients:** Give the right nutrients at the right times.
- **Space:** Allow enough room for each plant to grow; try not to overcrowd.

- **Stress management:** Reduce plant stress by giving it regular growing conditions and treating it with care.

6. TEMPERATURE STRESS SYMPTOMS:

- Heat stress: Burnt leaf edges, yellowing, and curling of leaves.

- Cold stress: dark leaves, purple stems, and slow growth.

Troubleshooting:

- **Temperature Monitoring:** Keep the ideal ranges of temperatures (58–70°F at night and 70–85°F during the day).
- **Cooling Systems:** To control heat, use fans, air conditioning, or exhaust systems.
- **Heating Solutions:** In colder regions, use heating mats or heaters.

7. pH IMBALANCES

Symptoms:

- Nutrient lockout: this occurs when nutrients are present but unavailable to the plant.

- Despite proper fertilization, there are general signs of nutrient deficiency.

Troubleshooting:

- **Testing pH:** Conduct routine pH tests on your water and growing medium.
- **pH adjustment:** To get the pH within the desired range, use solutions that are pH up or pH down.

8. ROOT PROBLEMS

Symptoms:

- Root rot: It is characterized by brown, mushy roots with an unpleasant odor.

- Poor plant growth and health.

Troubleshooting:

- **Appropriate Watering:** To avoid root rot, don't overwater.
- **Aeration:** Ensure enough drainage and aeration of the soil.
- **Root treatments:** To encourage strong root systems, use microorganisms or fungi (such as mycorrhizae).

9. HERMAPHRODITISM

Symptoms:

- Male and female flowers are produced by plants, which facilitates pollination and seed formation.

Troubleshooting:

- **Genetics:** To lower the chance of hermaphroditism, use premium, feminized seeds.
- **Stress Reduction:** Reduce the stress that plants experience as a result of factors such as nutrient imbalances, extreme temperatures, and light leaks.

- **Inspection:** Keep an eye out for hermaphrodite tendencies in plants and eliminate those that show them right away.

10. INFESTATIONS OF PESTS

Common Pests:

- Aphids

- Spider mites

- Whiteflies

- Fungus gnats

Troubleshooting:

- **Regular Checks:** Check plants often for signs of pests, like spider mite webs and aphid sticky leftovers.
- **Natural Predators:** Introduce predatory mites and ladybugs.

- **Neem Oil:** As a natural pesticide, use insecticidal soaps or neem oil.
- **Sanitation:** To reduce the number of pest habitats, keep your growing environment tidy and debris-free.

By resolving these typical issues with proper troubleshooting techniques, you can contribute to a successful and healthy cannabis grow. To identify problems early and maintain the health of your plants, regular maintenance and observation are essential.

Chapter Seven

Medical and Recreational Use of Cannabis

Cannabis usage has been increasingly popular in recent years, both for medicinal and recreational uses. Here's a summary of its medicinal applications, advantages, hazards, and status for recreational use:

Medical Usage of Cannabis

APPLICATIONS:

- **Chronic Pain Management:** Cannabis is frequently used to treat chronic pain, particularly in diseases like multiple sclerosis and arthritis.

- **Mental Health:** Although its effectiveness varies, it is occasionally used to treat depression, PTSD, and anxiety.

- **Cancer:** Pain, nausea, and appetite loss are just a few of the symptoms that cannabis can assist with.
- **Neurodegenerative Diseases:** Research indicates that people suffering from Parkinson's and Alzheimer's disease may benefit from cannabis use.
- **Epilepsy:** A few cannabis-derived medications, including Epidiolex, are licensed to treat severe and uncommon types of epilepsy.

The benefits include:

- **Pain Relief:** When other treatments have not worked, this method is helpful for many individuals with persistent pain.
- **Appetite Stimulation:** It helps patients who have lost their appetite due to conditions like HIV/AIDS or cancer treatments.

- **Anti-inflammatory:** The anti-inflammatory qualities of cannabinoids can aid in the treatment of a number of inflammatory diseases.

Hazards and adverse reactions:

- **Cognitive Impairment:** Extended use may cause memory loss and other cognitive impairments.
- **Mental Health Disorders:** Cannabis may occasionally make mental health disorders like paranoia and anxiety worse.
- **Abuse and Dependency:** Dependency is a possibility, particularly with strains that are THC-dominant.

Cannabis Usage for Recreation

Legalization and Status

- **Global Variance:** Cannabis laws pertaining to recreational use differ greatly. Some nations have decriminalized its usage, but others, like Uruguay and Canada, have completely legalized it.
- **United States:** Although it is still banned federally, recreational cannabis is allowed in a number of states, including California, Colorado, and Washington.

The benefits include:

- **Social and Recreational Enjoyment:** Many users report that cannabis improves social interactions and relaxation.
- **Economic Impact:** Legal cannabis markets provide jobs, increase tax income, and lower law enforcement expenses.

HAZARDS:

- **Health Concerns:** Smoking cannabis can provide respiratory hazards comparable to those associated with tobacco use.

- **Impaired Driving:** Cannabis usage can slow down response times and impair motor abilities, which raises the risk of accidents.

- **Impact on Youth:** Adolescents' early and extensive usage might interfere with brain development and cause cognitive problems.

Cannabis has been shown to have significant medicinal advantages, particularly in the treatment of chronic pain and other diseases. But there are hazards associated with using it, including possible dependency and cognitive effects.

Many areas are beginning to permit recreational usage more and more, and the main forces behind this trend are social and economic rewards. To ensure appropriate and informed usage, it is crucial to weigh these advantages against the hazards to one's health and safety.

Health Effects of cannabis: Short-term, long-term, psychological impact and physical health concerns

There are a number of short- and long-term psychological and physical health impacts of cannabis use.

SHORT-TERM HEALTH EFFECTS

Psychological Impact:

- *Relaxation and Euphoria:* Cannabis frequently results in emotions of relaxation, euphoria, and altered time perception.

- *Impaired Attention and Memory:* There can be major impairments to attention and memory in the short term.

- *Psychomotor Impairment:* Cannabis impairs motor abilities, response times, and coordination, which raises the possibility of mishaps.

- *Anxiety and Paranoia:* When using strong THC strains, some users may have increased anxiety, paranoia, or panic attacks.

Physical Health Issues:

- *Dryness of the mouth and eyes:* Users frequently report dry mouths (cottonmouth) and dry, red eyes.

- *Elevated Heart Rate:* Using cannabis may result in a brief elevation in heart rate.

- *Appetite Stimulation:* Cannabis, which is frequently seen as "the munchies," has the potential to enhance appetite.

- *Respiratory Issues:* The lungs may become irritated as a result of smoking cannabis, resulting in symptoms similar to bronchitis and severe coughing.

LONG-TERM HEALTH EFFECTS

Psychological Impact:

- *Mental Health Disorders:* Long-term use is associated with an elevated risk of mental health disorders, including depression, anxiety, and, in certain instances, psychosis and schizophrenia, particularly in individuals who are predisposed to these conditions.
- *Cognitive Decline:* The reduction of IQ and cognitive decline can result from the chronic, heavy use of cannabis, particularly during adolescence.

- *Addiction and Dependency:* Approximately 9% of cannabis users may have addiction and dependency as a result of cannabis use disorder.

Physical Health Issues:

- *Respiratory Issues:* Chronic cannabis smoking can result in respiratory problems that are comparable to those caused by tobacco smoking, such as chronic bronchitis and lung infections.

- *Suppression of the Immune System:* According to certain research, long-term cannabis usage may weaken the immune system, leaving the body more vulnerable to diseases.

- *Cardiovascular Problems:* Extended usage may raise the risk of heart disease and stroke, especially in people with underlying medical disorders.

ACKNOWLEDGEMENTS

God alone is worthy of all praise. In addition, I would like to express my gratitude to my amazing family, partner, readers, fans, friends, and customers for their unwavering encouragement and support.

www.ingramcontent.com/pod-product-compliance
Lightning Source LLC
Chambersburg PA
CBHW030558080526
44585CB00012B/419